HEALING LOVE
FINDING POWER

Joyce D. Sullivan

Abstract

The current book on love addiction has covered its potential neurobiological markers and its probable connection to specific attachment styles. However, further depth psychological investigations into the nature of love addiction—examining its etiology and mechanisms from a psychoanalytical or Jungian perspective, for instance—are almost nonexistent. This book utilizes a hermeneutic and heuristic lens to conduct a depth-based inquiry into the role of early experiences of ego development and attachment in the etiology of love addiction. It explores how the development of a Winnicottian false self likely led to the sequestering of contents of the true self in the Jungian shadow.

Drawing from psychoanalytical and Jungian theorists from Donald Winnicott and Carl Jung to Stephen Mitchell and Connie Zweig, this book asks how unconscious material can be recovered through depth-oriented clinical approaches to weaken the addiction and support the individual's journey toward wholeness.

Table of Contents

Chapter I   Introduction 1
   Area of Interest 1
   Guiding Purpose and Rationale 2
   Research Methodology 6
   Ethical Concerns 7
   Overview of book 8
Chapter II Review 9
   Attachment and Love Addiction 11
      Definition of Attachment Styles 11
   Codependency Versus Love Addiction 15
      Definitions of Codependency in the Field 15
   Obsession, Alexithymia, and Love Addiction 18
   Ethical Treatment of Love Addiction 21
   A Depth View on Love and Relationships 22
      Treatment of Love Addiction from a Depth Perspective ... 24
Chapter III Findings and Clinical Applications 27
   The False Self and Her Vulnerabilities 28
      Definitions of the True and False Self 30
   Anxious Attachment and False Self in Adulthood 32
      Definition of Jungian Shadow 37
   Summary of Findings 38
   Clinical Applications 40
      Overidentification with the Child Archetype 41
      Covert Narcissism in the Shadow 44
      Untapped Power in the Shadow 47
   Summary 51
Chapter IV Summary and Conclusions 53
   Conclusion 56
      Clinical Implications 57

Chapter I   Introduction

—

Area of Interest

Love addiction merits further exploration in psychological research, because it cuts to the vulnerable core of individuals and their attachment issues (Salani et al., 2022); can exact a large toll professionally, socially, and even physically (Earp et al., 2017; Sussman, 2010); and often cooccurs dangerously with other addictions (Griffin-Shelley, 2009). My personal struggles—as well as a possible causal relationship between certain maladaptive ego developments as viewed through a depth psychological lens and love addiction—inspired this exploration of the disorder. This book considers the etiology of love addiction as it relates to Winnicottian and Jungian models of psychic growth (Jung, 1939/1969, p. 275; Winnicott, 1965), while examining the unconscious traits that may be vying for recognition in the countless individuals bound by obsessive and self-destructive relationship-related thoughts and behaviors.

This book applies a hybrid hermeneutic and heuristic framework, buttressing its hypotheses with personal anecdotes that allow for a dynamic dialog between other researchers' findings and my own analysis. After passing through a long series of unfulfilling, triggering, and toxic relationships, I finally found my way to Sex and Love Addicts Anonymous (SLAA because the strictly co-dependent focus of Al-Anon felt off the mark for me. Co-dependency, defined as a focus on helping others and wanting to control them to the detriment of one's development (Lyon & Greenberg, 1991, was not my primary issue. I experienced other compulsive behaviors and thought patterns that accompanied sharp highs and lows within intimate relationships or spurred by unrequited romantic fantasies. For over a year, I dedicated myself to personal growth within SLAA. Gradually, I discovered more resources related to love addiction and came to see that it is an intractable and often destructive problem affecting many people. Additionally, I have now learned that the theories on the etiology of love addiction as well as treatment proposals are scant in the field's existing book.

Guiding Purpose and Rationale

Women and men who seem only to find partnerships or engage in relationships that consume them with obsessive thoughts or inspire detrimental, life-altering behaviors may face a two-fold problem of addiction and tragic loneliness. It seems human connection—a primary source of psychological comfort and fulfillment from infancy to death—can be perverted into something harmful when filtered through an insecure attachment system (Feeney & Noller, 1990; Levine & Heller, 2010) or other developmental twists. Put another way, addiction to pathological love serves as its own ironic barrier to genuine love and connection—and leaves a trail of heartbreaks that can result in depression and even suicide (Bolshakova et al., 2020; Sussman, 2010).

Founder of analytical psychology Carl G. Jung (1954/1969) opined that every psyche is striving toward wholeness (pp. 99–102). In his early work *Psychological Types*, Jung (1921/1971) defined the psyche as "the totality of all psychic processes, both conscious and unconscious" (pp. 463–464). He described psychic wholeness as an integration of the various parts of the Self: a transcendent entity comprising the psyche and all its potential, including that which exists in consciousness—the ego and persona— along with the psyche's unconscious contents, such as the shadow material that the ego has pushed out of conscious awareness (Stein, 1998). British psychoanalyst and child psychologist Donald Winnicott (1965), who followed in the footsteps of compatriot and pioneering child psychoanalyst Melanie Klein and her infant-focused object relations theory, developed a theory of ego development in babies based on whether the mothering they receive is "good-enough" or "not-good-enough" (p. 145–147, 177). Winnicott suggested that infants with not-good-enough mothers receive insufficient attunement to and accommodation of their needs in a crucial phase and instead learn to accommodate their mothers through compliance and hiding of the true self. Finally, British psychiatrist

John Bowlby's (1969) attachment theory regarding the infant–mother dyad established that purely relational needs exist. Canadian psychologist Mary Ainsworth and colleagues (1979) furthered Bowlby's theory by observing that infants who suffer from unattuned mothers develop either avoidant or anxious attachment styles. Others have shown that these styles shape one's relationships for life (Feeney & Noller, 1990; Salani et al., 2022). Gently surfacing repressed aspects of the love-addicted personality in a clinical setting and respectfully cooperating with clients (Griffin-Shelley, 2009; Smaldino, 1991) to

integrate those contents into consciousness is key to self-knowledge and Jung's

(1961/1963) concept of the "psychic development of the self" (p. 196).

This book examines how summoning from the darkness a client's unconscious, long-denied traits might help them achieve healthier relationships through increased selfknowledge. A heightened understanding of themselves will allow those individuals to reclaim personal power, and to feel more authentically autonomous in relationships and capable of accepting their own and others' realistic limitations. Assisting a person suffering from love addiction in exploring the roots of their overly accommodating behavior and anxious vigilance might help alleviate their shame (Griffin-Shelley, 2009) while elucidating and ideally reducing the potency of addictive patterns.

Given the likelihood of early trauma in the lives of love-addicted individuals (Griffin-Shelley, 2009), this book touches on the sensitivity required in helping a client peel away from addiction—and the vitalness of a supportive container in which to build ego strength (Mitchell, 1987; Smaldino, 1991) as they begin to see their relational motives more clearly. It also uses the author's personal experiences as a jumping-off point in exploring the etiology of love addiction.

This depth inquiry into love addiction could provide important information to the field of psychology, as the maladaptive effort to secure closeness and avoid abandonment at greater and greater costs is a common behavior, likely affecting at least 10% of the population (Temmrick, 1990). The research makes an important distinction between the concepts of codependency and love addiction, and highlights the trials and dangers of this widespread behavioral disorder that has no place in the *Diagnostic and Statistical Manual of Mental Illness* (*DSM-5*) to date (American Psychiatric Association [APA], 2013).

Examining love addiction's roots through a wide depth psychological lens also sheds light on the significant overlap between certain key psychodynamic and Jungian concepts.

Methodology

Statement of Research Problem and Research Question

Love addiction has undergone examination on a neurobiological level (Earp et al., 2017; Fisher et al., 2016; Redcay & Simonetti, 2018), but outside of correlations made to attachment style (Feeney & Noller, 1990; Salani et al., 2022), there have been few examinations of love addiction from a psychoanalytic (Smaldino, 1991) or Jungian perspective. The central inquiry of this book is as follows: What results of early attachment experiences precipitate the development of love addiction? How can unconscious material that was banished by the love addict early on be gently unearthed and reconfigured through depth-based clinical approaches to weaken the addictive cycle and serve the individual in becoming more self-aware and whole?

Definition of Depth Psychology

Depth psychology is a term coined by father of psychoanalysis Sigmund Freud's mentor Joseph Breuer (Meridien University, 2023). It refers to a branch of psychology that believes in the importance of the unconscious in shaping an individual, a point of view embraced by both Freud and Jung (Stein, 1998).

Research Methodology

Hermeneutic research inquiries are grounded in discovering what the research says that discredits preconceived notions, from which arises the development of more prejudgments for which confirmation or refutation is then sought. The key to hermeneutic investigations is seeking answers in the research and allowing those to lead to a more refined understanding (Moustakas, 1994, p. 10). Using a hermeneutic approach, this book looks carefully at what researchers have proposed for the associated traits and etiology of love addiction, comparing and contrasting their viewpoints and layering their conclusions with a depth perspective to arrive at a new hypothesis. At the same time, given my personal struggles with love addiction, a heuristic lens enables personal responses to and learning from the ideas encountered. It also allows for rich, first-hand material to echo and inform the hermeneutic inquiry.

According to heuristic research pioneer Clark Moustakas (1990), this methodology involves an internal search that provides an initial sense of meaning and context for the research inquiry, after which the research is allowed to cast new light on the self of the researcher (pp. 9–11). Moustakas described heuristic research as "a way of being informed, a way of knowing" (p. 10). He continued, "Whatever presents itself in the consciousness of the investigator as perception, sense, intuition, or knowledge represents an invitation for further elucidation" (p. 10).

The challenge of these approaches might be to offer an equitable, nonjudgmental platform for both the author's personal experience and the exploration of theoretical explanations and clinical applicability. However, this challenge is hardly insurmountable, and the tension therein should make for more vital, compelling work.

Ethical Concerns

Due to the history of trauma and strong sense of shame that many people with love addiction share, ethical treatment relies on a clinician's use of trauma-informed care and the recovery model (Yeager et al., 2013, pp.

388–391 and attention to transference and countertransference dynamics (Griffin-Shelley, 2009. Respecting boundaries and following ethical guidelines are also crucial to preventing re-traumatization.

The heuristic nature of this inquiry allows for the inevitable introduction of personal bias, especially without an explicit focus on the influence of cultural identity on the authors' findings. It should be noted that the author protects others' privacy by only including her own personal perspectives and experiences in the autobiographical material, and excluding any references to specific individuals from her past or present.

The risk also exists of ignoring socioeconomic and sociocultural influences on the relational behavior now defined by many as "love addiction." It is essential for practitioners to remain aware of differing cultural concepts of toxic, abusive, negligent, or over-sexualized relationships. This book includes a critical perspective on twelve-step programs for love addiction (Saulnier, 1996.

Overview of book

Chapter II reviews the book related to love addiction, attachment, and shadow work. Chapter III explores findings that illuminate the relationship of love addiction with shadow material and clinical applications related to the integration of the shadow in the treatment of love addiction. Chapter IV provides a summary and conclusion as well as suggestions for further research.

Chapter II Review

> As I burn up in your presence
>
> And I know now how it feels
>
> To be weakened like Achilles
>
> With you always at my heels
>
> —The Indigo Girls, "Ghost"

Love Addiction, Anxious Attachment, and a Depth Psychological Perspective

The field of psychology is still formulating a consensus on the definition of love addiction, which is not included in the *DSM-5* (APA, 2013) as a disorder. Recent researchers have joined in the field's ongoing debate regarding the definition of addiction as inclusive of compulsive behaviors like gambling, eating, and shopping versus strictly substance addictions. They have compared and contrasted love addiction with drug addiction and with the non-pathogenic highs and lows associated with new romance to determine its parameters (Earp et al., 2017; Fisher et al., 2016; Redcay & Simonetti, 2018).

Social psychologist Stanton Peele and psychiatrist Archie Brodsky (1975) coined the term in their seminal work *Love and Addiction*, defining love addiction as "a sterile, ingrown dependency relationship, with another person serving as the object of our need for security" (p. 13). Later, they discussed the ways that love addiction, as analogous to substance addiction, takes hold:

> The activity is reinforced in two ways—first, by a comforting sensation of wellbeing induced by the drug or other addictive object; second, by the atrophy of the addict's other interests and abilities and the general deterioration of his life situation while he is preoccupied with the addiction. (p. 27)

Peele and Brodsky's conception of love addiction was broader than most today, as they included any relationship that consumes the two parties and reduces their life options (p. 22), whereas most current definitions stipulate that the addiction manifests in unhappy relationships that have a significantly deleterious effect on one's life (Earp et al., 2017, p. 77). Psychologist Steve Sussman (2010) wrote that love is addictive when it is "(a) permeating one's daily life, (b) involving repeated out-of-control behavior, and (c) resulting in negative life consequences" (p. 32). Italian psychologist Alice Salani (2022) and colleagues defined love addiction as "a behavioral pattern characterized by a maladaptive and excessive interest toward a romantic partner, resulting in lack of control, the renouncing of other interests and behaviors, and other negative consequences" (p. 2).

Psychologist Brian D. Earp and colleagues (2017) considered contrasting theories of love addiction: the narrow theory posits that love addiction consists of abnormal, extreme love-related behaviors with correspondingly abnormal brain processes beyond the neurochemical reactions that normal love incites, and acquiescence to negative consequences; the broad view asserts that all forms of social attachment are addictive in driving us toward the reward of connection, but only require treatment when negative consequences arise (pp. 77–78). The authors did not favor one viewpoint, but asserted that with either perspective, treating the individual with a focus on their humanity and relationality rather than their potential love addiction is the most effective route (p. 89).

Attachment and Love Addiction

Following on the heels of initial theories of love addiction, researchers began inspecting the framework established by attachment theory (Ainsworth et al., 1978; Bowlby, 1969)—which asserts that all humans seek social connection for relational desires unnecessary to physical survival—and applying it to adult attachments. Psychologists Cindy Hazan and Philip Shaver (1987) inquired into the attachment systems of adults, concluding that a continuous thread connects infant attachment style— established by Ainsworth (1979) and colleagues—to later childhood attachment behavior, and adult forms of romantic attachment (Hazen & Shaver, 1987, pp. 512–513). Further, Hazan and Shaver collected data that supported their hypotheses regarding the quality and outcomes of securely versus insecurely-attached adults' romantic relationships based on factors like happiness, jealousy, trust, desire for reciprocation, and obsessive preoccupation (p. 515).

Definition of Attachment Styles

Throughout the 1950s and 1960s, Ainsworth (1970) conducted research based on

Bowlby's attachment theory that culminated in her Strange Situation Procedure. In that experiment, infants between 10 and 12 months old were observed being separated from their mothers and then reunited, with and without a strange adult present. Ainsworth (Tracy & Ainsworth, 1981) distilled the results to establish three primary attachment types among infants: secure, anxious/avoidant, and anxious/resistant—known more popularly now as secure, avoidant, and anxious-ambivalent (Feeney & Noller, 1990).

Building on prior research, psychologists Judith A. Feeney and Patricia Noller (1990) explored the connection between attachment styles and specific types of love.
Feeney and Noller attempted to bridge the gap between adult attachment styles and love addiction by investigating whether romantic love styles that feature love addiction behavior might be associated with a specific attachment style (p. 281). One of their hypotheses was that secure, avoidant, and anxious-ambivalent attachment styles would correspond with different love styles ("eros" or romantic, "ludus" or game-playing, and "mania" or possessive and dependent, respectively). They asked, "Can love addiction . . . be equated with anxious-ambivalent attachment?" (p. 282).

Whereas their study results did not confirm a clear correspondence between one attachment style and the mania or love addiction inventories utilized, Feeney and Noller (1990) did surface several findings regarding the anxiously-attached group. These subjects exhibited the lowest self-esteem, and the highest "intensity of love" experiences, of the three attachment styles (pp. 287–288). Their findings also showed that whereas avoidant and anxiously-attached individuals scored similarly on certain measures— including unfulfilled hopes, self-conscious anxiety, and personal and social self-esteem— the anxiously attached group showed the greatest dependence and desire for commitment; this was despite having the least enduring relationships (p. 287). Anxious subjects also stood apart in their clear endorsement of neurotic version of love involving preoccupation, emotional dependence, idealization, and possessiveness, over circumspect or companionate love (p. 289).

In studies, securely attached adults described their most important love relationship as "happy, friendly, and trusting" (Hazan and Shaver, 1987, p. 515) and reported accepting and supporting a partner regardless of their faults. By contrast, anxiously attached adults are prone to overtures that aim to keep their partners close at the hint of separation called "protest behaviors" (Levine & Heller, 2010, pp. 88–89)—a term coined by Bowlby (1969) to denote a child's responses to separation from its primary caregiver (p. 26). They are also prone to fretting over a partner's flaws that might drive a wedge between the two, frequently fearing but also anticipating abandonment, and overreacting somatically and relationally to the slightest sense of rejection (Gander & Buchheim, 2015; Hazan & Shaver, 1987; Levine & Heller, 2010).

In *Attached: The New Science of Adult Attachment and How it Can Help You Find—and Keep—Love,* psychiatrist Amir Levine and psychologist Rachel S. F. Heller (2010) discussed the seeming frequency of anxiously-attached and avoidant pairings. The authors cited studies showing that avoidant people actually seek partners who are anxiously attached. In addition, they posited that avoidant people are likely single and available more often than securely attached people, leaving the anxiously attached little choice but to couple up with avoidants. They warned that adults with anxious attachment risk becoming accustomed to, if not dependent on, the "emotional roller coaster" (p. 92) they experience with avoidant individuals: "After living like this for a while, you start to do something interesting. You start to equate the anxiety, the preoccupation, the obsession, and those ever-so-short bursts of joy with love" (p. 92).

Various surveys have been used to measure love addiction outside of attachment categories (Costa et al., 2021, p. 653). Italian Psychologist Sebastiano Costa and colleagues (2021) recently created an updated Love Addiction Inventory (LAI) with empirically established reliability. The LAI features four metrics for each of the six existing dimensions in the components model for behavioral addiction: salience, tolerance, mood modification, relapse, withdrawal, and conflict (p. 654). The 24 questions all begin with "How often do you," and include "How often do you feel abandoned when you're not with your partner?", "feel the need to increase the amount of time spent with your partner to experience pleasure?", and "leave your recreational and social activities to be in relationship with your partner?" (p. 656. Costa and his colleagues declared they based the LAI on the behavioral addiction components model and tailored it to love addiction to create "a useful assessment tool" (p. 666 containing reliable psychometrics characteristics.

Codependency Versus Love Addiction

Some discussion has appeared in the book about the overlap between codependency and love addiction (Bolshakova et al., 2020; Sussman, 2010). Whereas some authors and researchers have simply noted the likely cooccurrence of the two maladaptive behavioral patterns as discussed by research scientist Maria Bolshakova and colleagues (2020), others have insisted that the connection is still unknown (Sussman, 2010 or that love addiction is a subset of codependency (Mellody, 2002.

Definitions of Codependency in the Field

Codependency was conceived in the 1980s as a corollary to the disease model of alcoholism (Hogg & Frank, 1992, p. 371 and signified a learned behavioral system of psychological defenses and survival patterns in the family members of individuals with alcohol use disorders (Lyon & Greenberg, 1991, p. 435). Over a decade, the term became ubiquitous in popular psychological book, and, according to some, the definition bloated to include anyone who is now or once was in a dysfunctional relationship (p. 435). However, University of Arizona psychologists Deborah Lyon and Jeff Greenberg (1991) argued that it was not a late-20th-century concept but in fact was derived from what psychoanalyst Karen Horney in 1942 termed *morbid dependency*, which they describe as "the necessity of obtaining and preserving affection, even at the expense of engaging in a dependent, exploitive relationship" (p. 436).

Psychologists James Andrew Hogg and Mary Louise Frank (1992) noted that codependency has been defined frequently as encompassing the following characteristics: martyrdom, or sacrificing one's own needs for those of others; fusion, or giving up one's own identity in intimate relationships; intrusion, or control of other's behavior through manipulation, exploitation, or caretaking; perfectionism, or unrealistically high expectations of one's self and others; and addiction, or reliance on compulsive behaviors to regulate one's emotions (p. 371). In the major bestseller *Codependent No More: How to Stop Controlling Others and Start Caring for Yourself*, self-help author Melody Beattie (1986) wrote of her experience organizing support groups for the spouses of people with alcohol and substance use disorders: "I worked with women who were experts at taking care of everyone around them, yet these women doubted their ability to take care of themselves" (p. 2). Beattie described codependents' compulsion to help others whose lives were affected by substances, and even arrogance about their ability to do so: Most codependents were obsessed with other people.

With great precision and detail, they could recite long lists of the addict's deeds and misdeeds. . . . The codependents knew what the alcoholic or addict should and shouldn't do. And they wondered extensively why he or she didn't do it. (p. 2)

Popular addiction author and clinic founder Pia Mellody (2003) depicted love addiction as a subset of codependency in her work *Facing Love Addiction: Giving Yourself the Power to Change the Way You Love*. Mellody defined love addiction as being "dependent on, enmeshed with, and compulsively focused on taking care of another person" (p. 3). Regarding its relationship to codependency, Mellody added: While many assume that a codependent is someone who is dependent on, enmeshed with, and takes too much care of someone else, this condition is actually more properly called love addiction. Not all codependents make other people their Higher Power [like love addicts do]. Some wall themselves off from people; others offend and control without trying to be intimate. (p. 13)

Mellody described making someone else your "Higher Power"—a term used for the spiritual entity to which members surrender their control in twelve-step programs—as idealizing that person, or believing they have more power than you and will save you from the pain of life; she characterized this overvaluation of the other as the core issue of love addiction (p. 13).

Some love addiction theorists (Bolshakava et al., 2020) have asserted that different types of love addicts exist, with one of the types—more often female than male—particularly prone to co-dependency. This point conflicts with Mellody's (2003) argument that love addiction is a subset of co-dependency, and instead supports the theory that they are simply overlapping but separate disorders.

Obsession, Alexithymia, and Love Addiction

Some studies of harmful relationship-related thinking and behavior have focused on the obsessive preoccupation with relationships to which some lovers tend to succumb, refraining from considering a perhaps more controversial label of *love addiction*. Israeli psychologist Guy Doron and his colleagues (2013) investigated whether the confluence of attachment anxiety and over-reliance on romantic relationships for self-worth—which they called "double relationship-vulnerability"—predicts relationship-centered obsessions and obsessive-compulsive tendencies (p. 433). Their findings showed that attachment anxiety had a significant effect on relationship-oriented obsessive-compulsive symptoms, and that the effect was compounded when controlled for over-reliance on relationship for self-worth (p. 436). Topics causing preoccupation fell into three categories: feelings about one's partner, perceptions about a partner's feelings, and "appraisal of the 'rightness' of the relationship" (p. 435).

In a study of 344 Italian women, Salani and her research team (2022) examined the relationships between love addiction, emotional dysregulation, alexithymia, and child and adulthood attachment (p. 3). Their findings supported a theory that love addiction is a risk of childhood attachment failures; clinical subjects were more likely to identify their parents as only intermittently present and lacking an "empathic and affectionate parental attitude" (p. 16). They found that the women in love-addiction treatment reported a significantly higher incidence of preoccupied attachment, which in a four-factor attachment model advocated by social psychologists Kim Bartholomew and Leonard Horowitz "is characterized by negative models of oneself and high attachment anxiety, and positive models of the others and low avoidance" (Salani et al., 2022, p. 16). For these women, Salani et al. noted that "their sense of unworthiness fuels their deep need for closeness" (p. 16).

Salani and colleagues' (2022) examination of emotional dysregulation in love addiction revealed that "love addiction is characterized by . . . strong difficulties in coping with negative feelings like depression, loneliness, guilt, shame, [and] anxiety" (p. 12). Their theory on alexithymia held up in clinical results, proving that "love addiction ... could be associated with alexithymic aspects, implying a lack of awareness of one's emotions and difficulties in identifying and communicating them" (p. 14).

In discussing obsessive–compulsive personality organization as distinguished from obsessive–compulsive disorder (APA, 2013), psychoanalytic author Nancy McWilliams (2011) wrote that obsessive–compulsive personality types "idealize cognition and mentation" (p. 294). She observed:

> What especially strikes those of us who work with [obsessive-compulsive personalities] is that affect is unformulated, muted, suppressed, unavailable, or rationalized and moralized (MacKinnon et al., 2006). Many contemporary writers construe the obsessive allergy to affect as a type of dissociation. (p. 293)

Regarding their sense of self, McWilliams (2011) stated: "They are apt to be . . . hardworking, self-critical, and dependable . . . [Obsessive-compulsive individuals] worry a lot, especially in situations in which they have to make a choice" (p. 300). She went on,

"They may be equally nervous about giving in to lust, greed, vanity, sloth, or envy"; further, "both obsessive and compulsive people may be so saturated with irrational guilt and/or shame that they cannot absorb any more of these feelings" (p. 301).

In a chapter from *The Cambridge Handbook of Substance and Behavioral Addictions* entitled "Passionate Love Addiction: An Evolutionary Survival Mechanism That Can Go Terribly Wrong," Bolshakova, biological anthropologist Helen Fisher, and team (2020) stated that "those expressing an anxious-ambivalent attachment style were the most prone to *obsessive love; that is, love addiction* [emphasis added]" (p. 264). The authors also put forth a hypothesis about broad biologically-based styles of behavior and cognition triggered in part by neural systems that could lead to four different love addiction profiles: the "Explorer," fueled by dopamine, who is always looking for new experiences and excitement levels and has difficulty remaining in one relationship; the serotonin-fueled "Builder" who is overly concerned with safety and security; the testosterone-driven "Director" who uses aggression and violence to control a partner; and the estrogen-fueled "Negotiator" who is a strong empath, wants to nurture and understand others, has a heightened memory for emotional experiences, and is engaged by "theory of mind" (p. 264. The authors described typical Negotiators as "co-dependence junkies" who "obsessively analyze the partnership, as well as possess increased susceptibility to clinical depression and attempted suicide in response to romantic rejection" (pp. 264–265.

Notably, the fourth thinking style is the one that aligns with anxious attachment, which is most commonly linked to love addiction in the book. This unique correlation begs the question of whether the other "biologically-based temperament dimensions" (Bolshakova et al., 2020, p. 265).are more often seen in men, who are underrepresented in love addiction book due to the predominantly female study subjects.

Ethical Treatment of Love Addiction

In his essay "Ethical Issues in Sex and Love Addiction Treatment" published in the journal *Sexual Addiction & Compulsivity*, psychologist Eric Griffin-Shelley (2009 noted the unanimous view among his colleagues that "recovery from sex and love addiction is the most complex addiction recovery" (p. 34. He attributed this idea to the multiple addictions that sex and love addicts often maintain, and to the widespread history of trauma among sex and love addicts (p. 35. Griffin-Shelley wrote:

> Understanding a client's reenactment scenario is important in decoding [addictive] acting out . . . Recovery from other addictions focuses on more concrete triggers for relapse prevention, but, because sex and love addiction is an intimacy disorder, long-term recovery involves trauma resolution. (p. 35)

He stressed the imperative of a therapist's monitoring transference-countertransference dynamics, encouraging the discussion of feelings that arise within the therapeutic relationship, as well as maintaining awareness of one's own personal needs that may interfere with treatment (pp. 35–36). Griffin-Shelley contended that therapists should expect issues with authority among sex or love addictions (p. 36), and should handle boundary issues with the utmost care:

> [Sex and love addicts] tend to come from families that are either too distant, or detached, or too close or enmeshed (Carnes, 1991). Coming from families that are too rigid or too loose sets up the therapy relationship for conflicts around expectations, suggestions, and direction. . . . Clients' verbalizing these thoughts
> and feelings will help strengthen the therapeutic alliance. (2009, p. 38)

A Depth View on Love and Relationships

Although few have examined love addiction in the book, depth theorists have written about romantic or intimate relationships in general as prime territory for projection: the association of one's disowned and often unconscious qualities with another person (Desteian, 1989; Mitchell, 2002; Zweig & Wolf, 1997). In *Coming Together–Coming Apart: The Union of Opposites in Love Relationships*, Jungian analyst John A. Desteian (1989) defined romantic infatuation as a "finite period of passion" in which "we love our projections" as opposed to the "reality-oriented" state of love, in which we "love the person on whom we have projected" (p. 24). He identified the primary purpose of infatuation experiences as the rousing from slumber "of dormant parts of one's personality" (p. 23).

Desteian (1989) elaborated on this concept of infatuation and early love constituting an "awakening," a time when one's "essential spirit" constellates in the relationship and in one's views of the other, as opposed to being stifled by the "prevailing spirit" to which we all adapt, as dictated by our families and the culture (p. 35). In his view, these adaptations are made fundamentally out of fear of abandonment (p. 37).

However, Desteian contended that one's essential spirit is brought out in romantic love, even—or especially—in the stage of infatuation. "Essential spirit, the expression of a person's most intimate needs and desires, has a moving and transformative effect on lovers" (p. 37). Indeed, Desteian believed the primary function of our infatuations is to "begin the painful and arduous task of reintegrating" our essential spirit (p. 57).

Jungian analysts Connie Zweig and Steve Wolf (1997) shared Desteian's view of shadow projection as a driver of infatuation and romantic love. They wrote: "When we begin dating, as a natural part of development the shadow goes in search of its lost traits in others in an effort to recover the full range of our personality—the gold in the dark side" (p. 148). They saw this process as an unconscious compensatory effort. "Without our knowing it, the shadow is at work attempting to recreate early childhood relationship patterns with a secret mission—to heal old wounds and feel loved" (p. 148). It is to "the shadow's aim of completion" that Zweig and Wolf attributed the cliché "opposites attract": "optimists and pessimists, pursuers and distancers, extroverts and introverts" (p. 149). They argued that without awareness of these undercurrents, lovers become repulsed or enmeshed in the unclaimed parts of themselves they find in the other (p. 150).

Treatment of Love Addiction from a Depth Perspective

Clinical social worker Carol Smaldino (1991) drew from depth perspectives such as object relations theory to account for the "dreaded emptiness and dead-endedness" that often afflicts a love-addicted individual, and from which they look to the loved one as the sole escape route (p. 80). She attributed the dead-endedness to inadequate or disruptive childhood experiences:

> The steps of growth that pave the way for self-confidence and engagement with the outside world do not unfold but are instead thwarted. It is as though a sense of wonder is not returned by the

parent, leaving an emptiness and despair. The wonder, here, is particularly connected to the capacity for self-discovery, personal feelings, and personal capabilities . . . But sometimes the parent is wonderful . . .

The parent in this instant is in great need of being worshipped. (p. 82)

Smaldino (1991) emphasized the potent nature of the child's resultant love addiction, the "threat of breakdown revealed by a movement away from the addiction,"

and "the potential health in that breakdown" (p. 80). She described love

addiction as an urgency of perception that the substance craved (in this instance a person will obliterate the pain which otherwise remains. . . .The urgency of the feelings of need and craving returns again and again . . . [I]t can be consuming. At its most extreme, it can dominate all functioning. (p. 81)

Recent book on love addiction has revealed connections between anxious attachment, with its associated low self-esteem, and love addiction (Feeney & Noller, 1990. A possible etiology of love addiction, therefore, is materializing on the surface of a formerly murky lake of inquiry: this behavioral problem could stem from a lack of parental attunement that has led to an anemic sense of self-worth, spurring one to idealize others by comparison and to seek their closeness as reassurance when one feels lonely and inadequate (Doron et al., 2013; Smaldino, 1991). Another dimension of love addiction that has arisen repeatedly in the book is its correlation with obsessive preoccupation and concomitant alexithymia (Salani et al., 2022). When affects are not mirrored or are dismissed or rejected, one loses not only one's sense of entitlement to feelings but also basic awareness of them. Hence, alexithymia and preoccupied thinking are key components of both anxious attachment and love addiction.

Bolshakova et al. (2020) and Sussman (2010) offered many possible approaches to treating love addiction: twelve-step groups, cognitive-behavioral therapy, psychodynamic therapy, psychodrama group therapy, couples therapy, motivational interviewing, and pharmacotherapy. Sussman (2010) mentioned prevention techniques such as fostering a more secure attachment style through role play, direct instruction, or building into a school curriculum education about healthy relationships (pp. 38–39).

But why have feelings become so inaccessible to many love-addicted individuals? McWilliams (2011) suggested that when working with an obsessive–compulsive personality, "one way to bring a more affective dimension into the work is through imagery, symbolism, and artistic communication" (p. 306). A depth psychological view of love addiction might shed light on why an obsessively preoccupied lover has buried her feelings. It would likely point toward accessing a client's unconscious—which may house the feelings which have heretofore been inaccessible or hidden.

Chapter III Findings and Clinical Applications

So whilst our infant loves did grow,/

Disguises did, and shadows, flow/

From us, and our cares

—John Donne, "A Lecture upon the Shadow"

The False Self and the Shadow in Love Addiction

Much of the existing book on the etiology of love addiction centers on justifying its inclusion under the addiction umbrella based on neurobiological evidence (Earp et al., 2017; Fisher et al., 2016; Redcay & Simonetti, 2018), and establishing its affective and behavioral patterns (Bolshakova et al., 2020; Costa et al., 2021; Sussman, 2010. Aside from a select few studies on the correlation between love addiction and attachment systems (Salani et al., 2022; see also Feeney & Noller, 1990, psychodynamic or depth psychological examinations of love addiction (Smaldino, 1991—such as inquiries into the unconscious machinations of love addiction, or the value of incorporating the client's unconscious in love addiction treatment—are next to nonexistent. Hence, this book aims to investigate how reactions to early developmental experiences create vulnerability to love addiction, and how psychic material interred in the love addict's unconscious early in life can be reclaimed and integrated through depth psychological approaches to weaken the addictive cycle while supporting wholeness.   Building on book connecting love addiction to anxious attachment, codependence, and maladaptive behaviors like impulsivity and obsessive thinking, this book applies psychoanalytic and Jungian theory to examine how ego distortions resulting from a love addict's unconsciousness of fundamental personality components creates the ideal psychic landscape for love addiction to flourish. This chapter considers how the development of an overly compliant or codependent persona (defined below) in individuals with anxious attachment and love addiction obscures the true self. It looks at their tendency to cling to pseudo-innocence or pseudo-power (May, 1972) while remaining unaware of unconscious propensities such as childishness and covert narcissism, as well as assertiveness and personal power.

In its combined hermeneutic and heuristic approach to the analysis, this book allows the author to reference some of the relevant personal experience that lent an initial sense of meaning and context to this research. First-hand experience has remained relevant with my deepening inquiry into the topic—allowing for a dialog between research findings and personal history, and further elucidating the constellation of inter- and intrapersonal dynamics and psychic distortions that can foster love addiction.

The False Self and Her Vulnerabilities

In *The Maturational Process and the Facilitating Environment: Studies in the Theory of Emotional Development*, Winnicott (1965) claimed that a prerequisite of emotional maturity at any age is a person's ability to inhabit their relaxed, uncensored self in the presence of another person (pp. 29–31). He argued that this ability rests on the person's early experience of a acceptance through friendship or romantic connection, but I was sure that few could be trusted with my vulnerability. Revealing my dependence on another person was anathema to me and a sure source of shame. I wonder if this shame was rooted in a degree of unavailability of the adults around me, or their dismissal of certain of my complaints, emotions, and needs. In photos, I am always a smiling, sunshine-y baby. I recall being told at least once in my early childhood that I was unrecognizable when in a bad mood. I understood that I was a docile and sweet child who should not have—or express—difficult emotions. This seed of my Winnicottian false self would grow into a spirit-leeching ground cover that stymied my emotional development.

I tried to avoid making an unwelcome demand. I put on a happy face even when bored, angry, or hurt, allowing others a large margin of error. I did have needs, but I felt shame around them; I would have preferred to be alone than need something from another. My overarching goal in my first romantic forays—although I never achieved it for more than moments at a time—was to prove that I could maintain my grounding and autonomy in relationship with others, that I could become absorbed in my own thoughts or activities in another's presence. For me, it boiled down to optics: it was about making the other believe I was confident and unafraid of abandonment, regardless of the truth. My secret hope was that if I proved these things, I would secure their admiration and affection. I was exploiting myself, or my false self, in hopes of winning love. In "Ethical Issues in Sex and Love Addiction Treatment," Griffin-Shelley (2009) wrote:

> Unlike other trauma victims who tend to be overly needy, sex and love addicts act in a counter-dependent way *hiding their intense need for love and approval* [emphasis added]. This makes them hard to engage, isolative, avoidant, and preferring fantasy to real relationships (Leedes, 2001). With high levels of shame, these clients present with . . . denial, minimization, and projection. (p. 35)

Despite my identification with a false self—the always-smiling, slightly inhibited, never bored, needy, or insistent little girl—my underlying demands and cravings for love were vulnerable parts of my true self trying to push up through the soil. But a passionate, occasionally needful, fearful, or angry version of me had never felt safe above-ground, so I was not certain she really existed. Instead, I chose partners who exhibited these qualities, perhaps to a fault.

Anxious Attachment and False Self in Adulthood

Other theorists in Winnicott's time saw the clear influence that closeness with— and bonding capacity of—a primary caregiver has on an infant's behavior and development. Bowlby (1969) introduced his paradigm-shifting attachment theory to the psychoanalytic world based on observations of human and animal infants. Bowlby's theory held that a variety of behaviors on an infant's part are primarily social, with the goal of maintaining proximity to their mother figure, rather than simply fulfilling secondary drives for food or shelter (pp. 178–179). In *Volume I* of his groundbreaking work *Attachment and Loss*, Bowlby described "behavioral systems [that are] activated" (p. 179) by separation from the primary caregiver—activation which ideally dies down with the sight, sound, or touch of the mother. Bowlby observed that this attachment behavior is less readily triggered after age three, as cognitive developments make a child less needful of her mother's actual physical presence. However, he believed attachment behavior evolves over the years, and begins seeking new targets: "During adolescent and adult life yet further changes occur, including change of the figures towards whom the behaviour is directed" (p. 179).

Grounded in Bowlby's theories, Ainsworth's body of research (Van Rosmalen et al., 2015) revealed that securely attached babies feel great enough safety to stray from their mothers and explore while she is in the room, show distress when she leaves but happily reunite with her on her return (Ainsworth, 1979). By contrast, anxious/ambivalent infants seek proximity with their mother, anticipate her departure with distress, show acute anxiety while she is gone yet are ambivalent toward her upon her return, possibly displaying some anger. Unlike both other groups, infants with avoidant attachment style do not react when their mother leaves or returns—perhaps a defensive strategy to avoid painful feelings of rejection, given their elevated heart rates observed in later research (Van Rosmalen et al., 2015, p. 4)—and exhibit overt anger when she tries to pick them up or show physical affection (Ainsworth, 1979).

Again, key strategies associated with the false self are complying with the caregiver's wants and needs and hiding the true self (Winnicott, 1965, p. 9). If an infant with secure attachment style has a well-developed true self he or she is comfortable exposing to others, those with anxious and avoidant attachment styles utilize various

"secondary strategies to regulate the attachment system" (Gander & Buchheim, 2015,

p. 4). These adaptations are reactions to the primary caregiver's own attachment style and level of responsiveness and affection, and thereby limit the infant's ability to be authentic

among others. This jibes with Winnicott's (1965) description of false-self

> behavior: [W]here the mother cannot adapt well enough, the infant gets seduced into compliance, and a compliant False Self reacts to environmental demands and the infant seems to accept them. Through this False Self the infant builds up a false set of relationships. . . . [T]he child may grow to be just like mother, nurse, aunt, brother, or whoever at the time dominates the scene. The False Self has one positive and very important function: to hide the True Self. (pp. 146–147)

Winnicott's image of the false self is of a child who has relinquished her selfhood and begun to outwardly exist for others in order to satisfy the demands of her attachment system (Bowlby, 1969, pp. 372–73). In the face of impingement in the first years of life, an insecurely-attached infant finds relief when her compliant behavior elicits something like love. I propose that attempts to cope with the pain and low self-esteem of an underdeveloped true self prime the false self for codependence (Bolshakova et al., 2020) and addiction to a substance or person (Mellody, 2003).

Addiction is often the darker, more defended face of a compliant false self. Psychoanalytic psychiatrist and addiction specialist Frederic M. Baurer (2021) described a false self as an ideal host for addiction: "The true self is often buried beneath addiction, inaccessible. The addicted person is cut off from internal life, psychophobic, walled off within the false self persona . . . Addictive false self protects against [one's] vulnerability by offering pseudo-control" (p. 413). Baurer wrote of working with a substance-addicted client: "While out of control and destructive, she could live in this persona, this false self, and feel powerful in not caring. She could defeat her oppressors by passivity" (p. 415).

Passivity is likely to manifest in an anxious, overly compliant love addict, as well. People with love addiction occasionally act out by using protest behaviors—those common expressions of anxious attachment—such as drunk texting, reneging on important obligations to pursue or stalk lovers or exes, and other impulsive acts (Bolshakova et al., 2020; Sussman, 2010). However, they just as often turn to obsessive thinking. Obsessive thinking and rumination are considered marks of both anxious attachment and love addiction (Bolshakova et al., 2020; Hazan & Shaver, 1987; Fisher et al., 2016). Additionally, Winnicott (1965) wrote about a specific brand of false self "in which the intellectual process becomes the seat of the False Self. A dissociation between mind and psyche-soma develops" (p. 134). More apt to develop when caregivers are receptive to a child's non-emotional queries than their feeling states, this obsessivecompulsive false-self likely exhibits discomfort and avoidance around feelings and uses intellectualization as a coping mechanism. It is no surprise that some researchers have drawn a link between alexithymia (Salani et al., 2022)—the inability to identify one's own emotions—and love addiction.

In my own experience, my low self-esteem led me to fear presenting anything outside my false self to others, particularly in that most vulnerable and rejection-rife arena of romantic love. I would adjust my behavior to the sought-after love object, constantly trying to ease their difficult emotions at the expense of a full awareness of my own. When I managed to win a lover's affection with my pseudo-confident, easygoing false-self persona, I counted it as a victory and felt superficially gratified; I experienced a kind of high from the conquest. I was an obsessive thinker and fantasizer with a robust fear of rejection—making those first few and fleeting victories taste all the sweeter. I think I experienced each conquest as a reclamation of power after a markedly compliant childhood, ignoring the falsity of myself and of the power. The false self was a persona that I identified with and used to these ends; my true self remained shadowed.

My false self's conquests always failed as soon as the avoidant love object felt too hemmed in by my subtle but inevitable protest behaviors, yet I was convinced I would eventually learn the right formula for hanging onto an

avoidant other. This conviction, along with the intellectualization of my primal abandonment fears, seem to be markers of an intellectualizing false-self type and of many anxiously-attached love addicts. The question remains of where my primal fears of abandonment hid—along with my anger, and my true self's other contents—when a false self formed. Jung's (1946/1966) conception of the psyche's shadow as a storeroom or junk yard for parts of the individual
that have been semi-consciously severed is apropos here (p. 239).

Definition of Jungian Shadow

Jung's (1946/1966) most succinct definition of an individual's shadow was "the thing he has no wish to be" (p. 262). At times, Jung (1951/1971) described the personal shadow as housing the "dark," "negative" side of the personality, or the evil inside every individual (pp. 8–11). However, he viewed the shadow's contents as mixed. Jung
(1940/1969) wrote, "The shadow is merely somewhat inferior, primitive, unadaptive, and awkward; not wholly bad. It even contains childish or primitive qualities which would…vitalize and embellish human existence, but—convention forbids!" (p. 78). Stein
(1998) underscored this viewpoint: "Frequently shadow material is not evil. It is only felt to be so because of the shame attached to it due to its nonconformity with the persona" (p. 122). The false self could be seen as a kind of rigid or opaque persona, a front created by the ego for interfacing

with others (Stein, 1998). One is aware of their false self, even if they do not realize it is false, or understand that other parts of themselves—including their true self—are in shadow.

Desteian (1989) believed that the contents of our unconscious that begin to come to light in this consummation of the marriage of our essential spirit with another's in infatuation may be born from our shadow. "The term 'shadow' refers to those repressed personality traits that are part of one's personal unconscious . . . if we think of the ego as living in the full sunlight of consciousness, then the shadow lives in the ego's shade" (p. 55). Their residence in the ego's shade does not make these traits evil; in fact, they are part of our essential spirit, which is the expression of our most intimate needs and desires.

So how does a person begin to uproot or dismantle a false self persona, or reveal it for what it is? How can one resuscitate, rehydrate, and revive the true self so that it may re-start its stunted growth in adulthood? Additionally, what qualities or tendencies might commonly lie in the shadows of love-addicted individuals? The answers could reveal the most effective, empowering, and life-affirming approach to treating love addiction.

Summary of Findings

Winnicott (1965) held that in each person there exists the innate capacity to act organically and spontaneously without impingements. There is no *prima facie* moral value on this; it is simply freedom to access the true self, with whom a false-self persona has no real contact. Indeed, the same circumstances that have engendered a false-self profile have created an environment in which love addiction—like a cancerous growth— can take hold and thrive. These circumstances, according to my analysis, center on the lack of good-enough mothering that that would allow an infant to relax in the presence of another. Instead, the not-good-enough mothering creates anxiety about the mother's availability and compliance with a primary caregiver's needs rather than recognition and expression of the infant's own. The adult profile is of a codependent obsessive thinker who feels insecure around intimacy. They unconsciously seek the most emotionally bipolar intimate partnerships as those provide euphoric relief when non-forthcoming affection is delivered—and, in their painful times, hint at the chance of psychic healing. The love addict becomes addicted to the euphoric relief as well as to the hope of healing, and uses her well-worn skills of pretending and complying to maintain her addictive ties.

Jung (1921/1971) saw a person's psyche as encompassing a vast expanse of material and potential, including much that is outside of awareness. In *The Archetypes and the Collective Unconscious*, Jung (1954/1969) described the psyche as "a boiling cauldron of contradictory impulses, inhibitions, and affects" (p. 104). Wrote Jungian scholar Murray Stein (1998), "Some contents are reflected by the ego and held in consciousness. . . . while other psychic contents lie outside of consciousness, *for whatever reason or whatever duration* [emphasis added]" (pp.15–16). Development of a false self would mean rejecting some of psyche's potential as shameful or simply "notme." Jung (1946/1966) would say such rejected traits or tendencies have been driven into

the unconscious personal shadow (p. 59).

The goal of every human being, Jung (1939/1969) contended, is to achieve "individuation" (p. 275). He used this term "to denote the process by which a person becomes a psychological 'in-dividual,' that is, a separate indivisible unity or 'whole'" (p. 275):

> Knowledge of the phenomena that can only be explained on the hypothesis of unconscious psychic processes makes it doubtful whether the ego and its contents are in fact identical with the "whole." If unconscious processes exist at all, they must surely belong to the totality of the individual, even though they are not components of the conscious ego. (p. 275)

It is my contention that shadow material must be coaxed into the light of consciousness, and accepted in a nurturing context, for an individual to move forward on a journey of individuation. This may be the essential first step in knowing one's true self.

Clinical Applications

The compulsivity that comprises addiction—including love addiction's obsessions and exploits—often resides in the dark and shadowy, unconscious part of the psyche (Walker, 1994, pp. 35–36). As Baurer (2021) wrote,

"Addictive process is malignant . . . seeking external solutions to powerlessness and loss of control" (p. 407).

Whereas a person's outward social behavior in service of the addiction might arise from their false self, the addiction's underpinnings—such as impulsivity or insatiability—may reside in their shadow. If so, these tendencies share space with all other true-self characteristics the individual is hiding or defended against, due to shame and a clash with their persona. A clinical depth psychotherapist could help a client who has presented and used a false self in addiction in identifying and then integrating their shadow characteristics to further individuation. This process would support rediscovery of a precious and potent true self from which they were alienated early on, and of which they may have lost all concept. Shadow contents that may cost love-addicted individuals while hidden under the veil of denial include inflation of the child archetype (*puer* or *puella*) as well as covert narcissism and healthy personal power.

Overidentification with the Child Archetype

Jung (1951/1969) described archetypes as ineffable symbols whose images appear repeatedly across unrelated, disconnected peoples. He believed these symbols arise from an unconscious commons that he called the "collective unconscious" (p. 155). He argued that archetypes have potency in human psychology, even if their specific meanings are diffuse and ultimately elusive (pp. 152–153). Jung (1951/1971) also contended that projection, or the tendency of individuals with or without pathologies to see their own unwanted or hidden qualities in their significant others (pp. 9–10), is a method of identifying one's shadow material if the projection can be recognized for what it is. Jungian scholars have described projection of archetypal shadow material as common in close relationships, especially romantic pairings (Desteian, 1989; Zweig & Wolf, 1997).

According to Jung (1951/1969), the child archetype in the form of a young savior figure has surfaced time and again in humanity's collective unconscious (p. 157). "The child motif represents the precious, childhood aspect of the collective psyche," he wrote (p. 161). Jung conceded that a psyche's archetypal child may also represent forgotten bits of childhood that are nevertheless connected to a collective whole.

An individual who has complied with primary caregivers—for instance, by acting as a small husband or wife to their mother or father—may be harboring an overlyinnocent child archetype in their shadow. As an adult, they may find that when under emotional duress they identify with an exaggerated sense of innocence and goodness, nurse guilt when angry, and feel rejected by anything short of unconditional love. And although their false-self persona is mature, flexible, and understanding, a child archetype hidden in their shadow might lead them to project their fear of responsibility and commitment onto a partner. Again, individuals with anxious attachment have the shortest love relationships (Feeney & Noller, 1990), and people who tend toward obsessivecompulsive anxiety about relationships question the goodness and suitability of their partners constantly (Doron et al., 2013). This points to the illusions of perfection in love as well as the aversion to decisions and commitment of the child archetype.

My overidentification with the child or puella archetype has been, in my view, both an unconscious attempt at reclaiming something from the past that had been papered over or buried—both a playful innocence and unaffectedness that ideally would be met with unconditional love and an eternal grasping for a fantasy future defined by potential that escapes the confines of specificity, and is not anchored in reality (Jung, 1951/1969, p. 165). Nevertheless, for much of my adult life I would have denied or felt confused by an assessment that I was noncommittal, allergic to adult responsibility, or prone to dependency on others. These were the by turns attractive and repugnant qualities I saw in my partners. I believe that, had I understood my unconscious tendencies around this archetype, I might have fought to turn my rudder and right my ship sooner. Supporting the revelation of puer or puella overidentification in a love addict through a therapistpatient practice Jung (1958/1969) called "active imagination" (p. 68)— the use of such unconscious creations as "deceptions and lapses of memory" (p. 77), waking dreams, and

"spontaneous fantasies" (p. 78) to elicit the revelation of unconscious contents—as well as dream analysis and Socratic questioning could help them to identify and integrate this part of their shadow, reeling in their projections onto their addictive partner.

Covert Narcissism in the Shadow

In *Ego & Archetype: Individuation and The Religious Function of the Psyche*, analytical psychologist Edward F. Edinger (1972) discussed the ego inflation that accompanies an eternal childlike state—the *puer aeternus*—that some adults inhabit. Viewing themselves as forever in progress, they are unwilling or unable to reduce their options and commit to a specific—and finite—path in life. On some level this individual feels inflated and god-like, as if he should be able to do or have everything. Wrote Edinger: "He must give up his identification with original unconscious wholeness and voluntarily accept being a real fragment instead of an unreal whole. To be something in reality, he must give up everything *in potentia*" (p. 14).

The etiology of an individual's identification with a *puer aeternus* archetype may be a failure to transcend a primary narcissistic state, due to lack of parental mirroring and attunement. Psychodynamic psychologist Stephen Mitchell (1986) wrote about primary narcissism as viewed by psychoanalysts across time in his paper "The Wings of Icarus—

Illusion and the Problem of Narcissism." Freud and his successors considered narcissism to be a natural state infants inhabit when they perceive themselves to be the center of the universe, prior to understanding their separation as well as their fallibility (Mitchell,

1986, p. 108). In the primary narcissistic state, infantile illusions about one's self and others prevail. "Narcissism entails the attribution of illusory value," Mitchell wrote (p. 108), whether to one's self, another, or both. He elaborated:

> In Freud's view, withdrawal from reality is always perilous, the ultimate threat being the total loss of connection with the real world . . . and the less devastating threat posed by the vulnerable loss of self suffered by the unrequited lover, whose narcissism is transferred to the beloved and never returned. (p. 108)

It seems as if love addicts commonly project their own narcissistic shadow content onto real or fantasy partners, only to feel injured by the others' apparent self-absorption.

Mitchell (1986) discussed Winnicott's position on the necessity of a primary narcissistic state as revealed in his writings about infant omnipotence (p. 111). Winnicott (1965) tied omnipotence to the mother's facilitating environment, which allows babies the freedom to feel all-powerful or omnipotent and to view others subjectively, after which they gradually learn to accept the reality principle of perceiving others, or objects, objectively (p. 180). Winnicott considered this progression key to mature relations (Mitchell, 1986, p. 111), and saw subjective omnipotence as a crucial foundation to which older children and adults return in the act of creativity. Winnitcott (1965) argued that with a good-enough mother and a facilitating environment, an infant can eventually "abrogate omnipotence" (p. 146). Without good-enough mothering, a child might cling to

magical omnipotence, or the overvaluation of self or others.

    Mitchell (1986) noted that the "healthy narcissism" or subjective omnipotence that an adult can return to for generative activity reflects a "subtle dialectical balance between illusion and reality" (p. 120) in which illusions concerning oneself and others can be created, enjoyed, and relinquished when disappointments occur. In pathological narcissism, illusions are actively and consciously maintained; reality is sacrificed in order to perpetuate an addictive devotion to self-enobling, idealizing, or symbiotic fictions . . . In some narcissistic disturbances, narcissistic illusions are harbored secretly or repressed; the preoccupation with the limitations and risks of reality lead to an absence of joyfulness or liveliness (1986, p. 120). The last narcissistic type, more recently labeled "vulnerable" or "covert" narcissism (Rohmann et al., 2012), seems to track with the overthinker, the under-actor, the fantasizer: one who would rather vault herself onto a pedestal only in hidden or unconscious fantasies, yet would readily project her grandiosity onto her reciprocating or unrequited love object. A love-addicted individual believes in her own innocence and impotence to a great extent—or has become reliant upon the meager rewards his or her compliant persona gleans from relationships with avoidant or perhaps grandiose partners. In a study on narcissism in relationship, covert narcissists showed "preoccupation with grandiose fantasies, oscillation between feelings of superiority and inferiority, and fragile self-confidence" (p. 279).

An individual with love addiction must be helped to gradually uncover the narcissism in their shadow, and the illusions it creates about their own or another's infinitude—to shed light on their distorted views of themselves and their beloved, and also to release them from victimhood and addictive inclinations that owning such a shadow trait affords. As Zweig and Wolf (1997) stated in their popular work *Romancing the Shadow: A Guide to Soul Work for a Vital Authentic Life*:

> Denial is entrenched because the shadow does not want to come out of its hiding place. Its nature is to hide, to remain outside of awareness. So the shadow acts out indirectly…[or] it sneaks out compulsively, concealed in an addictive behavior.
>
> (p. 5)

Those with love addiction have entertained illusion to fight painful feelings of rejection and powerlessness (Smaldino, 1991). Hence, it is advisable to allow for some vacillation between reality and magical omnipotence within a safe and accepting therapeutic container before forcing a love-addicted person to adopt a more realistic lens.

Untapped Power in the Shadow

Zweig and Wolf (1997) wrote of a young woman who persisted in seeking relationships regardless of serially failed romances, maintaining the belief that if she could just correct some flaw in herself and become perfect, she would find love

(pp. 116-117). In their view, such a psyche's eternal flame of hope "pretends to be an authentic voice . . . but uses shields to defend against the appearance of the authentic Self, which lies hidden beneath the shadow" (p. 119). They proposed two questions to those with this pattern with the intention to uncover shadow material: "If you are single and ever hopeful, what loss do you defend against? What do you need to grieve?" (p. 119) I would add the following queries: "If you feel angry or disappointed, what do you do? How would you describe your love object in comparison with yourself? What is your experience of personal power?"

In his seminal work *Power and Innocence*, existential psychologist Rollo May

(1972) wrote, "The cooperative, loving side of existence goes hand in hand with coping and power, but neither one nor the other can be neglected if life is to be gratifying" (pp. 19–20). A love-addicted person has not yet enjoyed the maturity that comes with basic awareness of the shadow, whose contents, if made conscious, could both foster humility and cultivate self-efficacy and power.

It is common in dominant American culture that for women, personal power is equated with something ugly, dark, or negative (Rein, 2019), and relegate it to the shadow. In this sense, it is not only individual women's but also Western culture's collective unconscious that needs healing. Hence, a clinician's acknowledgment of the cultural constraints female clients have internalized—with a view toward intersectionality, or the sensitive consideration of multiple overlapping minority statuses—is imperative. Women may feel that embracing their personal power will make them unattractive and dominating or, worse, evil. As May (1972) put forth, there exists in every human life the potential for the power to be, for self-affirmation, and for selfassertion (pp. 40–41), and power is neither good nor evil (p. 122). Owning and asserting the power to be who they are may present the best opportunity for Western women to realize their individual potentials.

May (1972) also discussed the concept of "pseudoinnocence," (p. 49): in a word, a refusal to acknowledge one's own power and capacity for aggression:

> [American psychoanalyst Harry Stack Sullivan] believed that the feeling of power in the sense of having influence in interpersonal relations with significant others is crucial for the maintenance of self-esteem and for the process of maturity. When the sense of significance is lost, the individual shifts his attention to different, and often perverted or neurotic, forms of power. (p. 36)

In May's view, one needs to claim one's own power to live fully and healthily.

Paradoxically, this also means acknowledging one's vulnerability and powerlessness over other people, and one's addictions. Baurer (2022) asserted that addictive false self:

> protects against this vulnerability [resulting from early trauma] by offering pseudo-control, whereas the therapeutic relationship aiming for self-discovery threatens to expose emotional vulnerability, loss of control, and shame. We can expect countertherapeutic behavior as we uncover deep-seated shame, self-hatred, and fear of being known, but we proceed with empathy . . . We scan the therapeutic space for the often-faint voice of the true self as we aim to nurture this into consciousness. (p. 413)

Zweig and Wolf (1997) described collaborating with clients to uncover various powerful and mythical figures who dwell in their shadows, and can sometimes be seen only in what these clients project onto their love interests: a hidden but powerful Artemis who in her staunch self-reliance wants to roam free and hunt without responsibility or commitment, or Hera, the devoted and committed wife whose life revolves around her mate. They also addressed men who might unconsciously identify with Haephestus, Aphrodite's deformed husband who she banished from Olympus and who sought revenge in various ways, or Apollo, the god of dream and illusion, who while playing frolicking game with his male lover accidentally kills the partner off and then memorializes his loss, perhaps wanting the longing more than the satisfaction of a real lover.

The adult-child of the love addict must be nurtured by her therapist but also ushered onto a maturation path, by encouraging an authentic adult self to burst through the false self's confines. This might mean passing through an openly fiery, rebellious, and spontaneous puer or puella stage on the way to maturing; however, this stage need not comprise addiction or self-destruction. Rather than allowing the puer or puella fire to fuel a dark, all-consuming fire of passion, it needs a balance of earth and water: strength, rebirth, and spirituality. Hence, the puer or puella love addict begins to develop a grounding in power, responsibility and maturity: characteristics that have long been stowed in her shadow. She can then integrate the projections she has made on her lovers, using the reclaimed energy to burst forth as a genuine self who is primed for individuation.

Summary

Many of the primary psychic characteristics exhibited by love-addicted individuals—low self-esteem, anxious attachment, overly-accommodating or codependent personalities, obsessiveness, and alexithymia—are the identical qualities that appear when a false self develops in reaction to a lack of responsive resonance and accurate mirroring by an infant's primary caregivers. A false self has generally abdicated her personal power and sense of relational authenticity and autonomy in order to comply with the emotional needs and limitations of the caregiver, as the best hope for having her own needs met. The Winnicottian true self, those portions of the personality that felt shameful or unsafe in early attachment experiences, have not ceased to exist, but instead have been relegated to their Jungian shadow.

    I posit that such a trajectory describes the etiology of love addiction in its most common presentation. Jung (1951/1971) asserted that integrating shadow material is more than just a way to know oneself better but is requisite to a fully-realized, fulfilling life (p. 8). Drawing a love-addicted client's shadow material out through various forms of Jungian active imagination to uncover personality traits such as childishness, narcissism, and personal assertiveness will be by turns both humbling and empowering. Still, this work is likely to connect them more closely to reality, dismantling their projections onto idealizing and painful addictive relationships and clearing a path for true intimacy with others—including that "reality-oriented commitment and deep-rooted devotion" (Desteian, 1989, pp. 23–24) of real love.

Chapter IV Summary and Conclusions

Despite its absence from the *DSM-5* (APA, 2013, there has been some consensus that love addiction is a legitimate disorder (Bolshakova et al., 2020; Earp et al., 2017; that bears some relation to attachment styles (Feeney & Noller, 1990; Salani et al., 2022 and may create abnormal neurobiological effects in the vein of substance addiction disorders (Earp et al., 2017; Fisher et al., 2016; Redcay & Simonetti, 2018). Given the paucity of depth psychological voices in the book on love addiction (Smaldino, 1991), this book investigated why conscious and unconscious effects of certain kinds of early ego experiences seem to precipitate love addiction. Additionally, it considered how the love addict's true self—obscured in the unconscious early in life—can be surfaced and integrated in the therapy room to increase self-esteem, weaken the potency of addiction, and support the individuation process.

Initial love addiction theorists Peele and Brodsky (1975 broadly defined the disorder as the effort to objectify another for one's own dependency and security needs.
They aptly assessed that love addiction means allowing other areas of life to "atrophy" (p. 13 while focusing on the addictive relationship. Interestingly, they also described an individual who becomes lost in the security that their relationship provides, although more recent understandings do not associate love addiction with a sense of security. Attachment researchers Hazan and

Shaver (1987) discovered that anxiously-attached individuals are prone to adult romantic relationships marked by obsessive preoccupation.

Feeney and Noller (1990) found that insecure attachment styles—anxious and avoidant— endorsed the behaviors and thinking of love addiction. Anxiously attached individuals had the shortest relationships despite the greatest desire for commitment, and endorsed neurotic love involving preoccupation, emotional dependence, and idealization (Feeney & Noller, 1990). Bolshakova and colleagues (2020) have hypothesized that love addicts encompass avoidant types who perpetually seek the excitement of new lovers, aggressive and controlling types, and codependent types who have a tendency to focus on others' needs and problems and to struggle with asserting personal power in a healthy manner.

 A spate of publications (Earp et al., 2017; Fisher et al., 2016) has attempted to circumscribe love addiction within the established definitions of substance and behavioral addictions, as well as to develop a more precise emotional, cognitive, and behavioral inventory for measuring love addiction (Costa et al., 2019). Doron (2013) showed that the correlation between obsessive-compulsive relationship rumination and attachment anxiety becomes stronger when combined with reliance on partnerships for self-worth.

Alexithymia and love addiction have also been connected (Salani et al., 2022).

Discussions by depth psychologists of addiction—and love addiction in particular—have appeared in the book, although rarely. Baurer (2021) wrote about substance addiction and the false-self persona that supports the addiction by finding pseudo-power in addictive behaviors. Smaldino (1991 described the urgent and allconsuming nature of love addiction, given the high stakes of seeking one's self-worth in another. She also highlighted the strategic choice of partners in the love-addicted individual's "attempts to capture a sense of wholeness and healing that seem lacking anywhere else" (p. 81. Smaldino attributed this apparent lack to a failure in the infant's early development (pp. 82–83, when it is entranced by its own abilities and the greatness of its world. According to Smaldino, if the infant is not sufficiently supported in her delusions about self and others and their dismantling, he or she is left with a sense of abandonment, a constant fear of loss, and a vulnerability to shame (pp. 82–83.

Following the lead of the aforementioned depth-based queries, this book inquired into the traumatic ramifications of inadequate responsiveness from primary caregivers and the resultant false self. This book addressed the infancy stage of omnipotence (Winnicott, 1965, pp. 37, 57, when Winnicott believed the hiding of the true self occurs if the infant does not feel safe in self-expression. Alongside a heuristic examination of my experience, I also considered what role the hiding of the true self might play in feelings of impotence and low self-worth, covert narcissism, and over-valuation of others in relationships, all precursors to love addiction—and how the true self might be recovered. Finally, the book discussed how a clinician might help an individual reclaim from their Jungian shadow the contents of their true self lost in childhood as a crucial step in moving away from addiction and toward individuation.

Conclusion

Love addiction is a natural risk of the development of a Winnicottian false self who was forced to comply with primary caregivers, an adaptation that severed access to the true self. Once a false self with anxious attachment develops, what should have blossomed into the capacity for grounding and composure in the presence of others, expression of genuine feelings, and creativity becomes in love addiction the archetypal childishness and covert narcissism that projects its grandiosity onto love objects—while the person's true self lies estranged in shadow.

The projection of desired or shadow characteristics onto close relations or romantic partners is not unique to love addicts (Jung 1951/1971, pp. 9–10; see also Desteian, 1989), and may occur in veritably all intimate attachments. Depth theorists Zweig and Wolf (1997) declared that the stage of a relationship in which the couple embraces those projections is an immature stage in which the two coexist in an eggshell, until the shell cracks and they are able to see each other for who they are (p. 148).

Such a projection is likely more potent in love addiction, because the loveaddicted person has lost so much of their true self—and capacity for genuine expression—so early on. Such an individual's emotional growth and ability to inhabit reality was stunted during Winnicott's omnipotence phase of development, and a false self was created for protection, sowing the seeds of codependency as well as covert narcissism. As love-addicted individuals often exhibit an anxious attachment style (Salani et al., 2022), they are extra-sensitive to rejection by significant others, and find themselves both drawn to and spurned by the lost characteristics of their true selves they have sought and projected onto a partner, such as autonomy, creativity, self-efficacy, and expression of strong affects such as anger or sadness.

Uncovering her true self from the unconscious's shadowy territory would be invaluable to the love addict in recovery. By beginning to encounter their authenticity, love-addicted persons can start to relinquish false-self qualities like compliance, perfectionism, and moral superiority. Seeing with a clear eye the childishness and covert narcissism they harbor in their shadows will help to demystify and humanize the other.

Also present in the book was the use of a heuristic lens, which allowed me to explore from a personal perspective love addiction's psychological underpinnings. While writing, I began to consciously and unconsciously peer into my own shadow. To acknowledge my short-temperedness and criticalness within a relationship—and to not run from the truer intimacy that this entails—has afforded me tremendous growth.

Clinical Implications

Popular book on attachment and relationships (Levine & Heller, 2010) depicts the anxiously attached individual as characterized by hypersensitivity, and laments their mostly haphazard but painful couplings with avoidantly attached types who flee from commitment. Similarly, codependents are depicted (Lyon & Greenberg, 1991 as simply continuing a pattern of supporting and seeking esteem from unreliable partners that was learned in childhood.

However, I would assert that the dangers of addiction can be camouflaged within this seemingly just unfortunate phenomenon of anxious-avoidant pairings (Levine & Heller, 2010 in which one person puts forth more effort into loving connection, and the other distances. A surface analysis of this "opposites attract" dynamic belies possibly malignant issues: When an individual with a false-self persona and codependent tendencies attracts and chooses an avoidant or narcissistic partner, the false self projects their unconscious shadow traits, leading to toxic inflation of the other along with addiction to the highs and lows of their hard-won affection.

Along with other personality components that felt unacceptable in their infantile development, many love-addicted people carry narcissism in their shadow as a result of their primary caregivers' failure to deliver them safely and with care into awareness of reality's limitations. Covert narcissism demands a different treatment approach than what is oversimplified as anxiety around love attachments. It will be important to correct this blind spot in the field of psychology with regard to toxic relationships must be in order to properly treat individuals with love addiction. Individuals who find themselves in addictive relationships often have not landed there haphazardly: a two-way dance is in play, and the more passive partner has his or her own methods of exploiting both herself and others while covert narcissism creates a barrier to her capacity for genuine, limited, and imperfect connection. True expansion of the self can be achieved only by helping the individual begin to unearth and examine hidden or unconscious aspects of themselves through the use of night or daydreams, free writing, mythology, and art.

    Along with delivering a dose of reality, practitioners should take care to honor the dysphoria that may be both a symptom and a compulsion in love addiction. A lyric in the popular song "Somebody That I Used to Know" (Gotye & Kimbra, 2011) observes that one can become addicted to a certain kind of sadness, which seems all too true in love addiction. It is possible that with love addiction one has less control over the proliferation of triggers and associations. Social Worker Alex Redcay and psychotherapist Christina Simonetti (2018) observed, "All components of [the partner] and the relationship become triggers for the individual" (p. 84). This includes events, objects, songs and places you have been with that person (Bolshakova, 2020). Memories fuel fantasy, which provides a stable addictive supply even when comingled with the pain of heartbreak. As with other addictions, a focus on building ego strength by recognizing the individual's unrelated achievements and encouraging healthy thinking and activities (Baurer, 2021) in keeping with the recovery model (Yeager et al., 2013, pp. 388–391) is much more effective than just elimination of addictive behavior.

A Social Justice Perspective

Select studies (Saulnier, 1996) have highlighted the problematic potential of some 12-step addiction recovery tenets—for example, the promotion of the acceptance of powerlessness over "persons, places, and things" (p. 95)—when the audience includes minority groups, such as women of color. In her qualitative study on Black women identified as sex and love addicts, social worker Christine Saulnier (1996) asserted that promoting powerlessness among the white, heterosexual men who created Alcoholics Anonymous, the original 12-step group is appropriate, but could further marginalize and disempower groups who have experienced little sociocultural agency. Saulnier (1996) also argued that the 12-step model of attributing addiction to personal pathology is often limiting or even inaccurate when such problems "might preferably be described in political, or better yet, multidimensional terms" (p. 96). Twelve-step programs need not be championed by all counselors or recommended for every client. Feminist therapy, which embraces incorporating social marginalization in discussion of their presenting problems (Gehart, 2016, p. 415), or narrative therapy, which emphasizes externalizing a problem and considering its sociopolitical contexts (Nichols & Davis, 2021, p. 240), could be useful primary frameworks for all who struggle with addictive or abusive relationships, but particularly when considerations of intersectionality apply.

Areas of Future Research

Many potential facets of love addiction have yet to be explored in the book. Repetition compulsion as an impetus for seeking out emotionally unstable or codependent relationships should be investigated in relation to love addiction. The role of love addiction in abusive relationships needs to be investigated further. Equally important to explore is the development of obsessive relational orientation among adolescents. Qualitative or quantitative research should be done on the mechanisms of healing found through participation in 12-step groups such as SLAA for love addiction treatment. Within that fellowship, members refer to alternative iterations of love addiction, including addiction to non-romantic others for self-validation, which some book has touched on (Smaldino, 1991); however, these potentially-related maladaptive behaviors could be explored further. Finally, the efficacy of varying modalities in the treatment of love addiction— including narrative therapy, dreamwork, and grief and ritual therapy— should be investigated.

In Jung's view, bringing one's unconscious contents to consciousness is a large part of individuation (Stein, 1998, pp. 175–177), and integrating the shadow is key to this process (p. 122). Jung (1951/1971) wrote of the shadow's importance to psychic growth: The shadow is a moral problem that challenges the whole ego-personality, for no one can become conscious of the shadow without conscious moral effort. To become conscious of it involves recognizing the dark aspects of the personality as present and real. This act is the essential condition for any kind of selfknowledge. (p. 8)

While assisting love-addicted clients in separating them from the other's gravitational pull, shadow work may help the love addict shed the constricts of Winnicottian compliance and grow beyond the bounds of their own anxiously-attached, codependent persona. In this way, such clients may begin to finally enjoy the richness of their own personality and the satisfaction found in presenting this genuine face to the world.

www.ingramcontent.com/pod-product-compliance
Lightning Source LLC
LaVergne TN
LVHW020436080526
838202LV00055B/5208